# 12 DAYS OF

# CHRISTMAS

Published 2006 by

Veritas Publications
7/8 Lower Abbey Street
Dublin 1
Ireland
Email publications@veritas.ie
Website www.veritas.ie

ACTA Publications
5559 W. Howard Street
Skokie, IL 60077
USA
Email info@actapublications.com
Website www.actapublications.com

ISBN 1 85390 939 4
978 1 85390 939 9 (from January 2007)

ISBN 0 87946 319 8
978 0 87946 319 9 (from January 2007)

A catalogue record for this book is available from the British Library.

Designed by Bill Bolger
Printed in Italy

# 12 DAYS OF CHRISTMAS

Written by Kathleen Darragh

Illustrated by Jeanette Dunne

VERITAS

acta PUBLICATIONS

# on the first day of Christmas our true God sent to us...

## Our Saviour Baby Jesus

on the second
day of Christmas
our true God sent to us...
Two Caring Hearts...

and Our Saviour Baby Jesus

# on the third
# day of Christmas
# our true God sent to us...
## Three Wise Men...

2 Caring Hearts
and Our Saviour Baby Jesus

# on the fourth
# day of Christmas
# our true God sent to us...
## Four Shepherd Boys...

3 Wise Men, 2 Caring Hearts
and Our Saviour Baby Jesus

# on the fifth
# day of Christmas
# our true God sent to us...
## Five Christmas Carols...

4 Shepherd Boys, 3 Wise Men, 2 Caring Hearts
**and** Our Saviour Baby Jesus

13

on the sixth
day of Christmas
our true God sent to us...
Six Cards for Greeting...

Christmas Carols, 4 Shepherd Boys, 3 Wise Men, 2 Caring Hearts and Our Saviour Baby Jesus

on the seventh
day of Christmas
our true God sent to us...
Seven Presents for Giving...

6 Cards for Greeting, 5 Christmas Carols, 4 Shepherd Boys,
3 Wise Men, 2 Caring Hearts
**and** Our Saviour Baby Jesus

on the eighth
day of Christmas
our true God sent to us...
Eight Candles Glowing...

7 Presents for Giving, 6 Cards for Greeting, 5 Christmas Carols,
4 Shepherd Boys, 3 Wise Men, 2 Caring Hearts
**and** Our Saviour Baby Jesus

on the ninth
day of Christmas
our true God sent to us…
Nine Bells a Ringing…

8 Candles Glowing, 7 Presents for Giving, 6 Cards for Greeting,
Christmas Carols, 4 Shepherd Boys, 3 Wise Men, 2 Caring Hearts
**and** Our Saviour Baby Jesus

# 10

on the tenth
day of Christmas
our true God sent to us…
Ten Stars a Shining…

9 Bells a Ringing, 8 Candles Glowing, 7 Presents for Giving,
6 Cards for Greeting, 5 Christmas Carols, 4 Shepherd Boys,
3 Wise Men, 2 Caring Hearts **and** Our Saviour Baby Jesus

# 11

on the eleventh
day of Christmas
our true God sent to us…
Eleven Angels Singing…

10 Stars a Shining, 9 Bells a Ringing, 8 Candles Glowing,
7 Presents for Giving, 6 Cards for Greeting, 5 Christmas Carols,
4 Shepherd Boys, 3 Wise Men, 2 Caring Hearts
**and** Our Saviour Baby Jesus

on the twelfth
day of Christmas
our true God sent to us...
Twelve Children Praying...

11 Angels Singing, 10 Stars a Shining, 9 Bells a Ringing,
8 Candles Glowing, 7 Presents for Giving, 6 Cards for Greeting,
5 Christmas Carols, 4 Shepherd Boys, 3 Wise Men, 2 Caring Hearts
and Our Saviour Baby Jesus